Red Book 2

Phyllis Flowerdew

Oliver & Boyd

Illustrated by Shirley Bellwood, Jon Davis, John Harrold, Harry Horse, Annabel Large and Jim Ranson

Oliver & Boyd
Robert Stevenson House
1–3 Baxter's Place
Leith Walk
Edinburgh EH1 3BB

A Division of Longman Group UK Ltd

First published 1985
Fourth impression 1989

© Phyllis Flowerdew 1985
All rights reserved; no part of this
may be reproduced, stored in a ret
or transmitted in any form or by ar
electronic, mechanical, photocopy
recording, or otherwise without either the prior
written permission of the Publishers or a licence
permitting restricted copying in the United Kingdom
issued by the Copyright Licensing Agency Ltd,
33-34 Alfred Place, London, WC1E 7DP.

ISBN 0 05 003722 6

Set in 16/24pt Monophoto Plantin
Produced by Longman Group (FE) Ltd
Printed in Hong Kong

LEABHARLANNA ATHA CLIATH
SCHOOLS LIBRARY SERVICE
ACC. NO.   0050 037226
COPY NO. LS 4128
INV NO/90 4504
PRICE IR£   3.06
CLASS   R

Where to find the Stories

Page

- 4   Why Rabbit has a Short Tail
- 11 The Tree House
- 20 The Stream
- 31 The Inventor and the Plastic Man
- 42 Shaggy and the Storm
- 55 The Fossil Hunter

Why Rabbit has a Short Tail

In days of old,
so the Red Indians say,
Rabbit had a long tail,
long and fluffy and white.
He lived near a river.
It was wide and deep,
and it was the home
of a family of alligators.

One day Rabbit said to himself,
"I wish I could cross the river
and see what it's like
on the other side."

He couldn't swim across.
He couldn't jump across,
and there was no bridge
for him to run across.

So how could he get to the other side?

Then he had an idea.
He went to the bank of the river,
where the biggest alligator
was lying in the mud.

"Oh Grandfather Alligator,"
said Rabbit,
"how many alligators are there
in your family?"

"I don't know,"
said Grandfather Alligator.
"I can't count."

"I can count," said Rabbit.
"Shall I count them for you?"

"Yes please,"
said Grandfather Alligator.
He called all the alligators to him,
and said,

"Lie still, all of you,
so that Rabbit can count you."

"No, not like that," said Rabbit.
"You must all lie on the water
in a long line,
a nose to a tail,
a nose to a tail,
facing the other side of the river."

So all the alligators
lay on the water in a long line,
a nose to a tail, a nose to a tail,
facing the other side of the river.

Rabbit laughed to himself,
for they made a bridge
from one side of the river
to the other.
It was just what he wanted.

He stepped on to
the first alligator.
(It was the grandfather.)
He walked along his back
from the tail to the nose.
"That's one," he said.

Then he stepped on to
the next alligator,
and walked along its back
from the tail to the nose.

"That's two," he said.
Then he stepped on to
the next alligator
and walked along its back
from the tail to the nose.

"That's three," he said.

He went on like that,
all along the alligators' backs,
all along the line,
counting as he went.

Then he came to the last alligator.
It was the smallest one of all,
and it was feeling cross.
It was tired of lying so still
on the water, for so long.
It waited until Rabbit
was just stepping off its nose
on to the bank on the other side.

Then it lifted its head and snapped
at Rabbit's long, white tail.
It snapped it right off!

"You're playing a trick on us,"
said the smallest alligator.
"You're just using us for a bridge."

And from that day to this,
all rabbits have had short tails,
very short and fluffy and white.

The Tree House

In the summer holidays
Dad made a tree house
for Polly and Jim.
They played in it
all the week,
and had lots of fun.

In the house next door
lived an old man
called Mr Brown.
He was away that week,
but when he came home,
he looked out
of his kitchen window
and saw the tree house.
He saw Polly and Jim
and two of their friends
looking down at him.

"I don't like this at all,"
he said to himself.
"The children can see
right into my kitchen."

When Dad came home
from work that day,
Mr Brown knocked at the door.

"I don't like that tree house,"
he said.
"Your children and their friends
can see right into my kitchen."

"Oh dear," said Dad.
"I didn't think of that.
I'm sorry, Mr Brown.
I will have to take
the tree house down.
But the children have one more week
of holiday left,
so I hope you will let them play
in the tree house until Saturday.
Then I will have time
to take it down."

"Thank you," said Mr Brown.

So the children played
in the tree house
for one more week.
They were very sad
to think that Dad
would have to take it down.

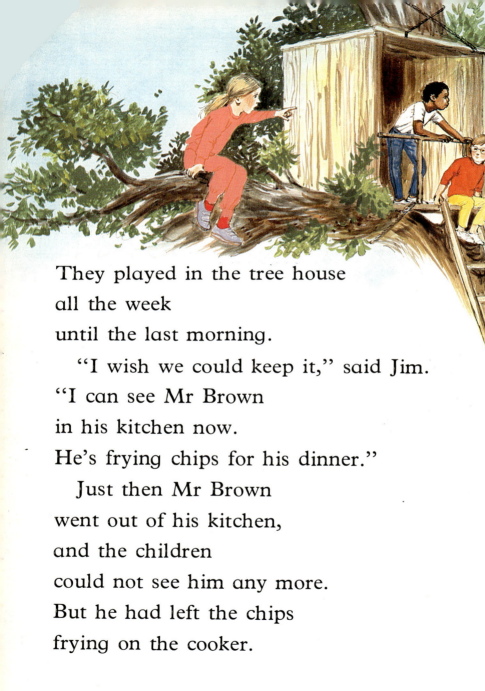

They played in the tree house
all the week
until the last morning.

"I wish we could keep it," said Jim.
"I can see Mr Brown
in his kitchen now.
He's frying chips for his dinner."

Just then Mr Brown
went out of his kitchen,
and the children
could not see him any more.
But he had left the chips
frying on the cooker.

Suddenly Polly saw a big flame leaping up in the pan.

"The chips are on fire!" she said.

"Oh!" said Jim.
"What a big flame!
We must call Mr Brown
before it sets the kitchen alight."

Down from the tree house
ran Polly and Jim.
They ran round
to Mr Brown's front door,
and knocked loudly on it.

"Your chips are on fire, Mr Brown!"
they said.
"Your frying pan is full of flames!"

Mr Brown ran into the kitchen.

By that time
the flames were higher still,
and a tea cloth had fallen
into the frying pan
and was burning too.
If he had been a little later,
Mr Brown's whole kitchen
might have been on fire.

When Dad came home
from work that day,
Mr Brown knocked at the door.
He held out a bar of chocolate
and a bag of crisps.

"These are for the children,"
he said, "and I don't want you
to take the tree house down after all.
I'm glad, now, that the children
can see right into my kitchen.
They saw my chips on fire today
and I think perhaps
they may have saved my house
from burning down."

"Yes. They told me about it," said Dad.
"Thank you very much, Mr Brown."

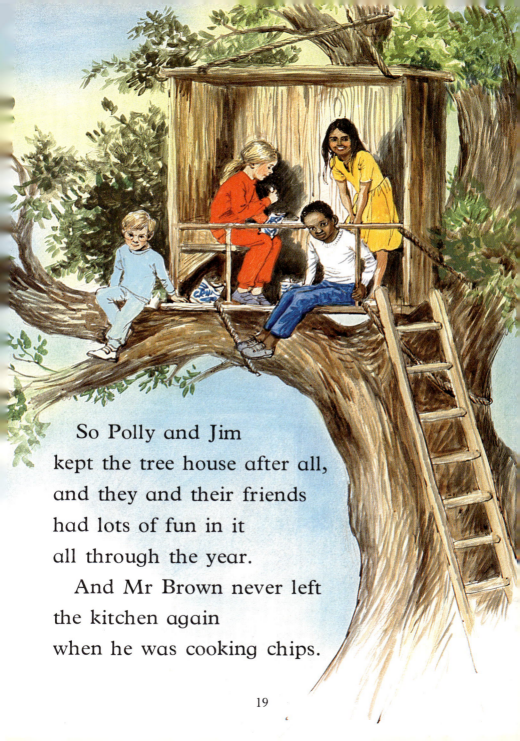

So Polly and Jim
kept the tree house after all,
and they and their friends
had lots of fun in it
all through the year.

And Mr Brown never left
the kitchen again
when he was cooking chips.

The Stream

Max lived in a wooden house
on the side of a mountain
in Switzerland.
A little way from the door
a small stream
went splashing by.
　It started
near the top of the mountain
and it brought down
little twigs
and fat fir cones
all bobbing along like boats.
　Max liked to poke at them
with a long stick,
and see how many
he could pull to the bank
and put on the grass.

Now, higher up the mountain
in a wooden hut,
there lived an old man
called Hans.
He lived up there
all the summer,
looking after his cows;
and the stream
went splashing by
outside his door too.

Sometimes he came down to the village past Max's house to buy bread.

One day he saw Max standing by the stream pulling out little twigs and fat fir cones.

He smiled and said, "You wait there at seven o'clock this evening, and I'll send something down the stream to you."

"All right," said Max. "I will."

Later, on the ground
near his hut,
Hans found
a funny twisted branch.
"Looks like a sea-serpent,"
he said,
and he took his knife
and cut off a bit here
and a bit there.
He carved a head
and two eyes and a mouth,
and there it was,
a small wooden sea-serpent.

Then at seven o'clock,
he called out,
 "Hallo! Hallo!"
and he sent it down the stream.
 Max waited.
He saw little twigs
and fat fir cones
bobbing along like boats.
 Then he saw a twisted branch.
Was it a twisted branch
or was it a sea-serpent?
He poked it with his stick
and pulled it to the bank.
He saw its head
and its eyes and its mouth.
 "A sea-serpent!" he laughed.

The next week
old Hans saw Max again.
"You wait there
at seven o'clock this evening,"
he said,
"and I'll send something
down the stream to you."
"All right," said Max.
"I will."

Now old Hans was very good
at wood carving,
and he had been busy
making a tiny boat
for Max.

So at seven o'clock,
he called out,
"Hallo! Hallo!"
and he sent it down the stream.

Max waited.
He saw little twigs
and fat fir cones
bobbing along like boats.
Then he saw a real boat,
a very small one,
and he poked it with his stick
and pulled it to the bank.

"What a fine little boat,"
he laughed.

The next week
old Hans saw Max again.
"Seven o'clock?" said Hans.
"Yes please," said Max.
Now this time,
Hans had a wooden bear
ready for Max.

He had carved it
most beautifully,
and it was standing on the table
in his hut.
   But the bear
didn't go down the stream
that day after all,
for poor old Hans slipped and fell
on the rocky ground
outside his door.

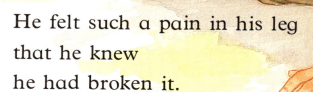

He felt such a pain in his leg
that he knew
he had broken it.
   How could he get help?

There was no phone.
There were no houses near.
  Then he saw the wooden bear,
and the bear gave him an idea.
He had some white paint
in the hut,
so he painted "Help Hans"
on a bit of flat wood.
Then at seven o'clock
he sent it down the stream.

  Max waited.
He saw little twigs
and fat fir cones
bobbing along like boats.
Then he saw a bit of wood
with big white letters on it,
saying, "Help Hans."

So Max was able to send help.
Old Hans was taken
to the hospital,
and his brother from the village
went up to the hut
to look after the cows.

Then at the end of the summer
when Hans was better,
he sent something
down the stream to Max.
It was the wooden bear
that had been waiting in the hut
all the summer long.

The Inventor and the Plastic Man

Peter's father was an inventor. He was always making things. Once he made a plastic man.

"He looks fine," said Peter. "but what can he do?"

"He can't do anything yet," said the inventor,

"but I will put some wires and screws
in his body,
and I will teach him
to do a lot of things.
First I will teach him to speak."

So the inventor
put some wires and screws
into Plastic Man's body,
and he made him speak.
Plastic Man said,
"Hallo. How are you?"
He said it very softly.

"That's fine," said Peter.
Then he and his father
left Plastic Man lying on the bed,
and they went out
to do some shopping.

When they came back there was a crowd of people outside the house.
There was also a police car and a fire engine.
A terrible noise came from the house.
It was the loudest shouting that anyone had ever heard.

Peter and his father rushed inside.
There they saw Plastic Man
lying on the bed
where they had left him.
He was shouting,
"Hallo. How are you?"
in the loudest voice
that anyone had ever heard.

Quickly the inventor
pressed a button
and twisted some wires,
and Plastic Man stopped shouting.
"Some wires were crossed,"
said the inventor.
"He'll be all right now."

The next day the inventor said,
"We will teach Plastic Man to walk."
So he put some more wires and screws
into Plastic Man's body,
and he made him walk.
Plastic Man walked slowly
and quietly round the room.
"That's fine," said Peter.
Then he and his father
left Plastic Man lying on the bed,
and they went out
to do some shopping.

While they were out
they saw a crowd of people
running into the park.
They were running, running, running,
and in front of them all
was Plastic Man,
running faster than anyone.

"Oh dear," said the inventor. "We must have left the door open."

"We shall never catch him," said Peter.

But a little later there was a big splash. Plastic Man had fallen into the pond. Peter and the inventor pulled him out of the water and carried him home.

The inventor pressed a button
and twisted some wires.

"I didn't mean him to run," he said,
"only to walk,
but some of the wires were crossed.
He'll be all right now."
And Plastic Man walked slowly
and quietly round the room.

The next day the inventor said,
"We will teach Plastic Man
to carry dishes from the table
and put them in the kitchen sink."
So he put some more wires and screws
into Plastic Man's body,
and he made him carry dishes
from the table
and put them in the kitchen sink.
Plastic Man did it quietly
and well.

"That's fine," said Peter.

Then he and his father
left Plastic Man lying on the bed,
and they went out
to do some shopping.

When they came back,
everything was quiet,
and Plastic Man was lying on the bed
where they had left him.
He was quiet and still.

BUT—
What was in the kitchen sink?

There were dishes and plates
and jerseys and jeans
and shirts and jackets
and boots and shoes
and toys and books
and bread and apples
and wellington boots!
The sink was piled up to the top!

"Oh dear," said the inventor.
"I didn't mean him to do that.
Some of his wires must be crossed."

The next day Peter said,

"What shall we teach Plastic Man to do now?"

"I don't think we will teach him anything else," said the inventor. "I think we will give him
a long, long rest,
a very, very,
long, long rest."

Shaggy and the Storm

Shaggy and Wolf-Dog
were running and playing
in the sunshine.
They went quite a long way,
and then Shaggy said,
 "The sky is growing dark,
and I think we shall have rain.
Wolf-Dog, we must turn back
and go home now."
 So they turned back
and started to walk home.
 At that very moment,
big drops of rain
began to fall,
and a wild, wild wind arose.
The sky grew darker

and thunder rolled and rumbled in the hills.
Rain fell faster and faster and lightning flashed.

Very soon Shaggy was wet all over, and Wolf-Dog's thick coat was dripping into little puddles all round him.

"Here," said Shaggy. "Let's shelter in this cave until the storm is over."

It was a small cave,
half hidden in the trees.
Shaggy and Wolf-Dog crept into it
and sat down on the sandy floor
and waited.

   They waited and waited
for the rain to stop
and for the wild, wild wind
to die down.
They waited and waited
for the thunder to end
and for the lightning to fade.

   They waited a long, long time.
Then suddenly
there was a great cracking sound
and a great crash
and a great shivering and shaking!

A big tree had blown down
in the wild, wild wind.
It had blown
right across the entrance of the cave,
and it blocked out
nearly all the daylight.

After a while the storm ended.
The rain stopped
and the wild, wild wind died down.
The thunder rolled away in the hills,
and the flashes of lightning
became fainter and fainter.
The storm was over.

"Good," said Shaggy.
"We will go home now."
But Wolf-Dog went to the entrance
of the cave,
and made crying noises,
a little like a wolf,
a little like a dog.

He sniffed with his nose
and scraped at the sand with his paws,
but he could not get out.
The fallen tree was lying
right across the entrance
of the cave.

Then Shaggy went to the entrance
of the cave.
He could see daylight
over the tree trunk,
but there was not enough room
for him to squeeze through.

He tried to push the tree away.
He pushed hard, hard, hard,
but he could not move it.

"Oh dear," he said.
"How shall we ever get out?"

Then Wolf-Dog went to the back
of the cave.

The cave was small and dark,
and Shaggy could not see
what Wolf-Dog was doing.
But Wolf-Dog made crying noises,
a little like a wolf,
a little like a dog.
He sniffed with his nose
and scraped at the sand with his paws.

He had found a small hole in the rock.
It was just big enough
for him to squeeze through
into another part of the cave.

Shaggy's eyes
were getting used to the darkness now,
and he saw Wolf-Dog slip away
in the shadows.

"Wolf-Dog!" he called,
"don't go away!
You might get stuck in the rock
or lost in the darkness.
Don't leave me here all alone.
Wolf-Dog! Wolf-Dog! Come back!"
But Wolf-Dog gave a yelp,
a little like a wolf,
a little like a dog,
and he was gone.

Shaggy sat on the sandy floor
and put his ear to the hole.
He couldn't hear Wolf-Dog now.
He couldn't hear
anything at all
except strange echoes in the cave.
He was all alone in the darkness,
and he was afraid
he would never see Wolf-Dog again.
He was afraid
he would never get out of the cave.

But Wolf-Dog was clever.
He sniffed all round the rocky walls
of the new part of the cave.
He sniffed with his nose
and scraped with his paws,
and soon he found
another small hole in the rock.

It was just big enough
for him to squeeze through,
and this time he squeezed through
into sand and grass and DAYLIGHT!

He shook himself
from his nose to his tail,
and then he ran and ran
till he came to the cave
where Shaggy lived.

Shaggy's mother and father
were standing outside
waiting for Shaggy to come home.

"He's a long time," said Mother.

"Here's Wolf-Dog," said Father,
"but Shaggy isn't with him."
Mother patted Wolf-Dog.

"Where's Shaggy?" she said.
"Where's Shaggy?"

Wolf-Dog walked a little way
and then came back.

He walked a little way again and then came back.

"He wants us to follow him," said Father.
So Mother and Father followed Wolf-Dog, and he led them to the cave.
There they saw the tree lying across the entrance.

They pulled it and pulled it,
and moved it just enough
to make room for Shaggy to climb out.

He was very glad to be free.

"Thank you. Thank you," he said.

"Wolf-Dog is very clever," said Father,
and Wolf-Dog gave a loud yelp
because he was so pleased.

The Fossil Hunter

Zoë lived near the sea
in Suffolk.
She liked walking along the beach
looking for shells and pebbles.
There were round pebbles
and flat pebbles,
brown ones and white ones,
washed smooth by the sea.
She liked to feel them,
cold and shiny in her hand,
and best of all
she liked the bits of amber.
These were yellow or orange,
clear and bright like the sun.
    She looked for fossils too.
She had looked for them
since she had been five years old.

Sometimes there were fossil shells
or bits of rock
with strange patterns on them.
Sometimes there were bits
that looked like scraps
of fossil bone.

She began to collect them
and set them out on a shelf
in her bedroom,
as if it were a museum.

Then one day
when she was eight years old,
she went out in the car
with her mother and father
and her little sister.
They drove through farmland
and woods
to a small country church.
They left the car there
and they walked along a footpath
down to the beach.

It was a fine spring day,
and a cool wind was blowing.
Zoë stood still
and smelled the fresh salty smell
of the sea.
She looked up at the high cliffs
and across the beach
of sand and pebbles.

"Now where shall I start looking
for fossils and amber today?"
she thought.

Soon she was down on her knees
picking up pebbles
and scraping away
at little patches of sand.
Her mother and father walked along
at the edge of the sea,

and her little sister
started a game of her own.

Time passed quickly.
Zoë turned over broken shells,
and picked up trails of seaweed,
and felt smooth, shiny pebbles
in her hand.

Then suddenly she saw
something rather unusual.
It wasn't a pebble.
It wasn't a bit of bone.
It wasn't a piece of amber.
It was a strange shape,
and it was heavy like stone.

It was shiny and smooth
and a little like tortoiseshell.
It had a number of colours in it—
black and brown and yellow,
and some specks of green.

A fossil!
It must be some sort of fossil!

"Daddy," said Zoë,
running over to him,
"what do you think this is?"
Her father looked at it
and turned it round
and felt it.

"It's a tooth," he said.
"Look, it's worn smooth on top,
and these are the roots below."

"What animal do you think
it belonged to?" asked Zoë.

"Something big," said her father.
"Perhaps a rhino, long, long ago."

This was exciting—
to think of a big animal
like a rhino
walking near this quiet beach
long, long ago.
Zoë could hardly wait for Monday
so that she could take the tooth
to school
and show it to her teacher.

Zoë's teacher took the tooth
to the museum
in the town near by.
   "They say at the museum
that it's a horse's tooth,"
she told Zoë,
"and it could be a million
or even two million
years old.
It was a different kind of horse
from those that live today.
It was more like a zebra,
but perhaps without the stripes.
   And the people at the museum say
that if you would give them the tooth,
they would like to put it on show."
   So it was a horse's tooth!
It had belonged to a horse
that had disappeared from the earth
hundreds of thousands of years ago.

Zoë's picture was put in the paper.
She was smiling
and holding the fossil tooth.
Even the big London papers
printed a few lines
about her exciting find.

It was quite hard for her
to settle down
to school work again.
She kept day-dreaming about her horse.
She thought of it
running in the wind, happy and free.

She thought of it
rolling in the rough grass
so long, long ago.
    She would like to have kept the tooth
and put it in her bedroom
with her shells and pebbles and fossils,
but she gave it to the museum
so that hundreds of other people
could see it too.